Poo

KNEW?

Poo
KNEW?

Some stuff you might find interesting,
astonishing, and amusing about poo

EMMA ROYDE AND ALEX PARSONS

DOG 'n' BONE

Published in 2014 by Dog 'n' Bone Books

An imprint of Ryland Peters & Small Ltd

20–21 Jockey's Fields   519 Broadway, 5th Floor
London WC1R 4BW   New York, NY 10012

www.rylandpeters.com

10 9 8 7 6 5 4 3 2 1

Text © Emma Royde 2014
Design and photography © Dog 'n' Bone Books 2014

A CIP catalog record for this book is available from
the Library of Congress and the British Library.

ISBN: 978 1 909313 47 7

Printed in China

Editor: Tim Leng
Designer: Geoff Borin
Cartoon illustration: John Riordan
Additional illustration: pages 6, 7, 13 (top), 17, 18, 28, 34 (center),
35, 38, 39, 41, 42, 43, 45 (top), 54 © iStockphoto.com

For digital editions, visit www.cicobooks.com/apps.php

Contents

Introductory crap

You're probably expecting some kind of smelly, farty, funny stuff about embarrassing moments and piles of shit, but the world of human waste is not all fun and games. Some people, it's true, find poo and sewers a generally hilarious topic, while others are moved by the magnificence of crap and all things associated with it. Here are some thoughts to cherish:

"Unlike other body-related functions like dance, drama, and songs, defecation is very lowly. Yet when discussing it, one ends up discussing the whole spectrum of human behavior, national economy, politics, role of media, cultural preference, and so forth."

Dr. Bindeshwar Pathak, Indian sanitarian

"IN SPITE OF ALL MAN'S DEVELOPMENTAL ADVANCES, HE SCARCELY FINDS THE SMELL OF HIS OWN EXCRETA REPULSIVE, BUT ONLY THAT OF OTHER PEOPLE'S."

Sigmund Freud from his book *Civilization and Its Discontents*

"The material itself is as rich as oil and probably more useful. It contains nitrogen and phosphates... It can be both food and poison. It can contaminate and cultivate. Millions of people cook with gas made by fermenting it... I don't like to call it 'waste,' when it can be turned into bricks, when it can make roads or jewelry."

⨾⨾

"HOW A SOCIETY DISPOSES OF ITS HUMAN EXCREMENT IS AN INDICATION OF HOW IT TREATS ITS HUMANS."

⨾⨾

"All the world's great faiths instruct their followers how best to manage their excrement, because hygiene is holy."

Three quotes by **Rose George**, author of *The Big Necessity: The Unmentionable World of Human Waste and Why It Matters.* A very wise woman.

"THREE STONES ARE ENOUGH TO WIPE ONE'S ARSE."

Greek proverb

"Shit is a more onerous theological problem than is evil. Since God gave man freedom, we can, if need be, accept the idea that He is not responsible for man's crimes. The responsibility for shit, however, rests entirely with Him, the creator of man."

Milan Kundera, *The Unbearable Lightness of Being*

"Sex is interesting, but it's not totally important. I mean it's not even as important (physically) as excretion. A man can go 70 years without a piece of ass, but he can die in a week without a bowel movement."

Charles Bukowski

Chapter One

True Shit

People are full of shit

Everybody shits, and everybody farts: kings and queens, paupers and princes, popes and presidents, dictators, democratically elected leaders, and the general mass of humanity. This is because every human being has a gastrointestinal tract in which gases form and stuff gets sorted and shifted. And what gets shifted is a good indication of what's going on inside us, and that is what concerns us here.

What's in a turd? 75% water, unless we're talking diarrhea or constipation, 8% dead bacteria, and another 8% of indigestible stuff like cellulose or corn kernels—this is the fiber that provides the traction to get crap moving through the intestines. What remains is a mix of fats such as cholesterol, inorganic salts like phosphates, live bacteria, dead cells, mucus from the lining of the intestine, and protein.

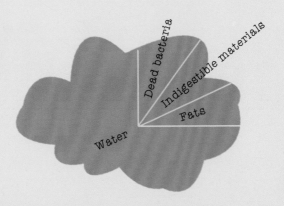

The **amount of crap** that one human being produces in one day varies depending on diet. The average Western person with access to fatty fast food and lots of protein will dump around 8.9 oz (252.3 g) of waste per day. That's 200 lbs (90 kg) in a year and, say this average person enjoys 70 years of adult life, that's a lifetime load of 14,044 lbs (6.37 metric tons) of absolute crap. But Asians, who eat a whole lot more fiber than Westerners do, can produce almost three times as much on a smaller intake. Which is a good thing, healthwise.

Drink lots of water and eat loads of turnips and Brussels sprouts, and you too could produce a **monster poo**.

Releasing a large amount of crap can give you a **light-headed crap "high"** as toxins leave the body. Enjoy!

Normal **crapping frequency** ranges from three times a day to three times a week.

General observations

And now for the science bit...

If you see **blood in the lavatory bowl**, do not immediately panic. If it is bright red, the cause is likely to be piles, or a crack in the anus. But if bleeding persists, call your doctor. Dark blood, which comes from high up the digestive tract, results in a purplish-black and sticky-looking poo, and **should be investigated at once**.

Post-binge-drinking craps are often explosive as your body attempts to purge toxins from your system. This is because ethanol, present in alcohol, has a stimulating effect on the bowel, pushing the contents through speedily so there's less time to absorb the liquid. Apart from signing the pledge, you should drink loads of water and lay off dark spirits like brandy. Stick to the vodka.

Crap **stinks** because it contains bacteria, which produce smelly, sulfur-rich organic compounds, and the inorganic gas hydrogen sulfide which smells of rotten eggs. It's an interesting fact that hydrogen sulfide is one of those gases that causes olefactory fatigue at high concentration, so after a while people can't smell it any more. Which explains why you may think your toilet smells lovely after you've left it, but the next person needs a gas mask.

From tasty mouthful to end game, as it were, is **a journey of just over 30 ft (9 m)**. Your small intestine, which does the job of supplying lively bacteria to break down organic matter, is about 23 ft (7 m) long and 1 in. (2.5 cm) in diameter. Your large intestine, or colon, where feces gather to have the water leached out, is about 5 ft (1.5 m) long with a diameter of about 2 in. (5 cm).

And **how long will it take?** Swallowing takes about 10 seconds, then food sloshes about in the stomach for about three to four hours. The journey through the small intestine takes about three hours, and then it's colon time, which can last about two days.

Doing the math on the **food to crap ratio** requires a calculator, but basically means our bodies need an awful lot of food just to regenerate and keep going.

The **amount of food** eaten by the average person in a lifetime in the UK is 78,264 lbs (35.5 metric tons). However, if you look at American data, food consumption for the same lifespan is reckoned to be 138,891 lbs (63 metric tons)—nearly twice as much. Which is not a good thing.

> "What on earth would I do if four bears came into my camp? Why, I would die of course. Literally shit myself lifeless."

Bill Bryson, *A Walk in the Woods: Rediscovering America on the Appalachian Trail*

To sharpen performance on the pitch, the track, or the boardroom, a relaxing **pre-game dump** is highly recommended. An empty colon means you can run faster, jump higher, and think more clearly—the perfect way to prepare mentally and physically for a stressful event. A word of warning to all athletes: make sure you know your way out of a lycra skinsuit before visiting the bathroom.

Proof positive that empty bowels speed you along. In a heightened state of terror, the sympathetic nervous system goes into overdrive to prepare the body for fight or flight. In the acute stress response, adrenaline is pumped through the system to boost heart and lung activity, blood vessels dilate in muscles needed for fighting and fleeing, while parts of the body not needed in an emergency, such as the tear ducts and salivary glands, as well as erections in men and elimination control, shut down. Bladder and bowels "let go," so you can get the hell out of there, albeit with crap in your pants.

Be wary of colonic irrigation—it's not what it's cracked up to be, and is often carried out by practitioners with no medical training. Filling the colon with water and sluicing out the contents may seem like a brilliant idea, but it confuses the natural movements of the bowel and the delicate balance of bacteria in the gut, and can cause cramping, bloating, nausea, vomiting, electrolyte imbalance, and in the worst case scenario, kidney failure. There are far simpler and cheaper ways to achieve colon health: eat a balanced diet, exercise regularly, get six to eight hours of sleep, and have regular medical check-ups.

The **color of crap** comes mainly from a pigment that arises from the breakdown of red blood cells in the liver and bone marrow, and may or may not have something to do with iron. The whole process is extremely complicated and actually quite tiresome to explain, but there you go: shit is brown.

Or not, as the case may be. **Black, tarry crap** can be the result of taking iron pills or bleeding high up the digestive tract. **Green crap** is either due to overloading on spinach or green food coloring, or iron pills. **Yellow crap** indicates the presence of fat and is a symptom of pancreatic disease. **Dark red crap** is often the disturbing result of eating too much beetroot. **Blue crap** in children can come from blue food coloring such as cake icing. Intense red food coloring can produce **bright red crap**. Sometimes **brightly colored foods** pass through the gut almost unchanged, resulting in a turd that may be speckled with bright red fragments, such as peppers, or bright yellow kernels of corn.

Gas

A crucial ingredient in the make-up
of your poo.

A poo with an unusually high gas content will **float** in the toilet bowl, defying all efforts to sink it or flush it away. Sometimes the gases produced by bacteria in our gut don't have a chance to emerge as a discreet fart, but remain in the feces—this gas-filled item has a lower density than water.

☙

Hot spices— particularly black pepper, red pepper, and chili— do no harm to the stomach lining or the intestines but the oils they contain do **retain the burn** right through the gastrointestinal system. These oils can also generate hot farts.

☙

The intestine is quite a gassy environment: gas is produced by chemical reactions in our guts, and by the bacteria living inside us. It even seeps in from our blood and enters our body as we breathe. Eventually, it's all got to come out somewhere… **For the chemically-minded**, a fart is made up of nitrogen and carbon dioxide from the air we breathe (the oxygen having been absorbed by the blood), an extra helping of carbon dioxide from the chemical reaction between stomach acid and intestinal fluids, and hydrogen, smelly hydrogen sulfide, and methane produced by bacteria doing their job.

Farts

No matter how sophisticated you might be, farts are never ever not going to be funny.

Noxious smells emanating from the rear end are caused by hydrogen sulfide and a mildly toxic, very smelly crystalline compound called skatole (or C_9H_9N), a substance occurring naturally in feces, coal tar, and, in low concentration, in some plants and flowers. **Skatole** is really interesting stuff: apart from the word itself, on which all manner of things scatological are based, this naturally occurring compound is used as a fixative in perfume, in the manufacture of stink bombs, and (in its synthetic form) in ice cream.

More about smelly farts. The problem is sulfur, so the more sulfur-rich your diet, the more sulfides and skatole will be produced by the bacteria in your guts, and the more your farts will stink. Stink-producing foods include meat, boiled eggs, and cauliflower. Beans, so often held up as the villain of the piece, fart-wise, produce large amounts of not particularly stinky gas: this is because beans, along with cabbage, peppers, and surprisingly, raisins, contain indigestible sugars that really excite the bacteria in the guts, producing large amounts of gas as a result.

A low-pressure environment like an airplane can cause the gas inside you to expand, so refrain from cabbage and beans if contemplating a transatlantic flight.

Noisy farts are no more stinky than silent ones. Rather like the embouchure of the trumpet player, the noise is made by vibrations in the opening, and the volume depends on the relationship between the velocity of expulsion and the degree of tightness of the muscles.

What if everyone in the world farted at once? On average, one adult farts about 14 times a day, producing about half a liter of gas.

People who swallow a lot of air fart more than people who don't. **There's a reason your mother told you not to eat with your mouth open!**

"*Nothing is worse than to finish a good shit, then reach over and find the toilet paper container empty. Even the most horrible human being on earth deserves to wipe his ass.*"

Charles Bukowski

"Sanitation is more important than independence."

Mahatma Gandhi

"HE IS SO RICH, HE HAS NO ROOM TO SHIT."

Marcus Aurelius, *Meditations*

Chapter Two

Miscellaneous Crap

Farting fun

Who would have thought the gastrointestinal tract, with all its gurglings, rumblings, explosions, surprises, and ultimately satisfying end result would provide so much entertainment? Here's some more crap about crap.

Here's an opening your careers' advisor may have missed: **The professional flatulist, or farter**. The most famous and most successful was Joseph Pujol, known as *Le Pétomane*, which basically means farter in French. He was born in Marseille in 1857 and first became aware of his "talent" as a young boy while swimming in the sea—he took a deep breath before diving and felt sea water rushing up his bum which later cascaded out. Working on his abdominal control, Pujol was eventually able to suck up both air and water into his colon and push it out with considerable force. He did have a day job as a baker, but it was farting that brought him fame and fortune, not his bran muffins.

Le Pétomane's act at the Moulin Rouge started off with fart impressions: beginning with a newly-wed's timid toot before moving on to bird song, whistles, cannon fire, and thunderstorms. All in the best possible taste, I think you'll agree. Pujol would then step discreetly offstage and insert a rubber tube in his bum, which emerged from a hole in his elegant, well-cut trousers. He used the tube to smoke cigarettes, blow out stage lights, and, after attaching a flute to the end, he would drive the audience into a frenzy by farting popular sing-along tunes. His wind was said to be virtually odorless. Pujol gave up professional farting while at the top of his game and returned to baking. He died in 1945 at the age of 88, but his reputation lingered on like the smell on the landing.

Le Pétomane may have been the most famous, but he was not the first. *The City of God*, a philosophical treatise written halfway through the first millennium A.D. by **Saint Augustine**, mentions some performers who possessed "such command of their bowels, that they can break wind continuously at will, so as to produce the effect of singing."

The **professional farters of medieval Ireland** were called *braigetori*. As entertainers, they ranked at the lower end of a scale headed by storytellers and harpists.

Let's hear it for **Roland the Farter**, jester to King Henry II, who was given a manor house in Suffolk. His annual rent was an obligation to perform *Unum saltum et siffletum et unum bumbulum* (one jump, one whistle, and one fart) at Court every Christmas.

Now you know the Latin for fart.

BUMBULUM

is a splendid word and deserves much wider exposure. Tell your friends.
Start a trend.

Farting amusingly at parties was a quality much prized among entertainers in 14th century Britain.

The Roman Emperor Claudius passed a law **legalizing farting at banquets** out of concern for people's health. There was a widespread belief that a person could be poisoned or catch a disease by retaining farts.

Why fart? **The word fart** comes from the Old English word *feortan*, of echoic origin, which means that the word was chosen to sound like the action.

A **Dutch oven** is what you create when pulling the covers over the head of the person you are in bed with while farting. Some people get off on this.

Legendary modernist architect **Le Corbusier** considered the toilet to be "one of the most beautiful objects industry has ever invented."

The average human being spends
three years of their life on the toilet.

What do you call it? The English will ask for the lavatory, the toilet, the ladies, the gents. Americans will, confusingly and euphemistically, ask for the bathroom, the restroom, the john, or the can. Australians head for the dunny. In most of Europe some version of toilet will be understood, as will WC, which stands for water closet.

Where's the toilet?

Here is the phrase in a random hand-picked selection of totally useless languages:

Scots:

Whaur's the lavvy?

Swahili:

Choo kiko wapi?

Luxembourgish:

Wou ass d'Toilette?

Latin:

Ubi sunt latrinae?

Pshitt!

Mistakes can easily be made when searching for that perfect brand name with global reach. Pity the French company (Perrier, actually) who marketed Pshitt!, a perfectly delicious lemonade drink, to the English-speaking world, or the bright young things who dreamt up the Mitsubishi Pajero, a word that means wanker in Spanish. To avoid similar pitfalls, here's the translation of shit in a variety of tongues:

Albanian
MUT

Azerbaijani
POKH

Basque
KAKA

Bosnian
SRANJE

Czech
HOVNO

Danish
LORT

Dutch
KAK

Estonian
SITT

Finnish
PASKA

French
MERDE

Gaelic
CAC

German
KACKE

Greek
SKATA

Haitian Creole
PUPOU

Hungarian
TAT

Icelandic
SKIT

Indonesian
KOTORAN

Italian
CACCA

Japanese
KUSO

Javanese
PAWARTO

Latin
PUPPE

Latvian
KUGA PAKALGALS

Lithuanian
KAKOTI

Malay
TAHI

Mexican
MOJON

Norwegian
BÆSJ

Polish
KUPA

Portuguese
POPA

Romanian
RAHAT

Russian
KAKASHKA

Slovak
LODNÉ ZADOK

Slovenian
KAKEC

Somali
QORMAYO

Spanish
MIERDA

Swahili
KINYEZI

Tagalog
TAE

The world's going down the toilet

An insight into international porcelain.

The **most expensive toilet in the world** is a solid 24-carat gold throne in "The World's Most Expensive Gold and Jewelry Sparkling Environmental Friendly Washroom" in the showroom of the Hang Fung Gold Technology Group in Hong Kong.

❧

WC's of the world. It may come as something of a surprise, but they're not all the same due to the fact that every country has a different concept of hygiene, access to disposable paper, and water. The average British/American white porcelain loo is located indoors in a purpose-built room, is about 16 inches (40 cm) off the ground, with a rim, a seat, a lid, a flush lever, a handy dispenser of aloe-vera-impregnated, softly quilted, three-ply loo paper, and what goes in disappears with a bit of a splash in a pan of water. In Germany, Austria, Denmark, and the Netherlands there will be a shelf perched daintily above water level, so every dump can be inspected and admired. Some countries suffering from inadequate drains and paper shortages offer no toilet paper. Instead, there are water spouts at the back, just below the rim, or failing that a hose and bucket. What to do? You squirt the water, shake your booty, wipe with your left hand, and hope for the best. Squat toilets, a challenge for those with bad knees, are the norm in many eastern countries. They are, in fact, a good thing as the squatting angle is more fit for purpose, as if that is any comfort as you emerge with trembling thighs and shit on your shoes. And, for something really gross, there's the pig toilet—basically a squatter with an ingenious chute leading directly to a pen of hungry pigs… please, no! **ENOUGH!**

Crapping in space is difficult. A fancy, wrap-around, wearable port-a-loo device bristling with suction tubes and sensors is in development, but the reality for most working astronauts is the nappy. On the Apollo 7 mission, astronauts had to tape a bag to their rear end, then reach into the bag to grab the emerging turd as there's no gravity up there to do the work for them. They then had to open up a capsule of blue germicide and mush everything together. Crew members' advice? "Get naked, allow an hour, have plenty of tissues ready." Still want to be an astronaut?

South Korea

Not content with producing some of the world's finest technological inventions, South Korea is also a nation obsessed with shit.

Cheers!

Picture the scene: you've just arrived in Seoul, South Korea, for the first time and you're really excited to be there. You decide to celebrate with a drink, so head to the nearest bar you can find. But what's good to drink in Seoul, what do the locals enjoy? A beer maybe; or a glass or wine? A cocktail, perhaps? You ask for the drinks menu and your eyes skim the list until you spot something called `Ttongsul`. It sounds pretty authentic and you decide to give it a try. Bad move. Ttongsul is actually a tasty beverage consisting of Korean rice wine mixed together with the fermented shit of a little kid, ideally aged between four and seven for the finest flavors. Hmmmm, delicious!

This is definitely a concoction not for the faint-hearted, rivaling even the most vicious dirty-pint combinations any group of university students could come up with on a big night out. Thankfully, Ttsongsul is actually pretty rare these days, and there are only a few living devotees still making the drink today. It was originally used for medicinal purposes, with users believing it could cure anything, from bruising to broken bones, and heal infections. So, if you ever find yourself in Seoul on a night out and you've fallen over drunk, think twice before you accept the kind help from a stranger offering to give you something to help with the swelling.

Kids these days

Collecting is a big part of a child's life, with many hours spent in the playground doing deals and trades with friends to amass an even larger collection of marbles, Pokémon cards, action figures, or badges. So far, so normal. In South Korea, however, kids prefer to ditch the latest season of football trading cards and instead collect little models and stickers of "cute poops," which are smiling, happy little drawings of turds. And the fun doesn't stop there. At some shops you can even buy cakes and donuts shaped to look like doodoo. Delicious.

THE CRAP MUSEUM

Not content with producing the world's shittest drink, South Korea is also home to the Suwon Toilet Museum, the only museum in the world dedicated to the crapper. The museum complex consists of Mr Toilet's House, a 4,500 square foot building in the shape of a giant toilet, which contains a visitors' center where locals and tourists can learn about all things lavatory-related.

Valuable crap

One man's shit is another man's treasure.

Human excrement does make good fertilizer, eventually. Our hunter-gatherer ancestors would dump human waste into piles well away from the cave/tent living area and thus discovered the waste-to-fertilizer process, as the dung heap turned into fertile soil for their crops. The Sumerians and Romans hired delivery boys to carry crap in "honey wagons" to nearby fields for fertilization. Crap from latrines was euphemistically termed "night soil," as it was removed under cover of night by the humblest of workers so as not to offend the wealthiest of crappers. The Chinese put a higher value on "night soil" from wealthier households as rich people's crap contained more nutrients due to their better diets.

Not that long ago, doctors took crap very seriously and **examining stools was a vital diagnostic tool**. There's an engraving dated about 1860 of a doctor examining a bedpan with real intensity and a cheeky maid asking him whether he'd like a fork. The fascination with feces knew no bounds: doctors prescribed excrement to be eaten, drunk, or rubbed into the skin.

A pinch of **health-giving snuff anyone?**
A dried and powdered form of human excrement, called *poudrette*, was sniffed by the grandest ladies of the 18th-century French court.

Martin Luther, the religious reformer, reputedly **ate one spoonful of his own feces every day**, stating that he "couldn't understand the generosity of a God who freely gave such important and useful remedies."

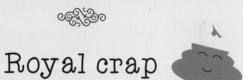

Royal crap

You had to be there… King Louis XIV would **receive foreign dignitaries while having a crap**. In a similar vein, President Johnson apparently invited reporters and his staff into the can while he was crapping. What kind of an ego is that?

More on presidential poo. If the President craps anywhere outside the American sewage system, Secret Service agents are under orders to collect it. This is so that foreign powers can't **hijack the crap** and analyze it for information on the President's health. Did they really sign up for this?

Dead crap

Not a dignified way to go...

Elvis Presley didn't exactly die on the loo as is often believed; he was actually slumped a few feet away with his trousers round his knees, having made an attempt to crawl for help. The coroner pronounced that Elvis had died "in an incident on a commode." Cause of death was first given as a heart attack. He was obese, suffered from glaucoma, high blood pressure, liver damage, a history of abusing prescription drugs, and had a massively enlarged colon. Elvis suffered from chronic constipation, however, and according to Dr George Nichopoulos, the singer's doctor for the last 12 years of his life, that is what killed him.

There are various versions of the death in 1796 of **Catherine the Great**, renowned leader of Russia. Perhaps the most dignified is that she died grunting on the toilet; the worst is that she was crushed to death while having sex with a horse. Take your pick.

Early on June 22, 1969, **Judy Garland** stumbled to the bathroom where she took, according to the coroner, "an incautious overdose of barbiturates." Time passed until husband Mickey Deans woke up around 10:30 and, finding Garland wasn't in bed, knocked on the locked bathroom door. After getting no response, Deans climbed in the bathroom window and found the troubled legend perched on the toilet, stiff with rigor mortis. She was 47.

King George II was not a well man. Fat, deaf, German, and shaky on his pins, he drank a hot chocolate and then went to the loo. Moments later a crash was heard, and the king was pronounced dead from "overexertions on the privy." It was October 25, 1760.

Lenny Bruce died while shooting up heroin, naked, on a toilet. Perhaps not how you'd wish to be remembered.

Saxon monarch **Edmund Ironside** was stabbed in the bum by a Viking hiding in his toilet or, as a later chronicler put it: "Edmund was shown into a privy rigged with a drawn bow with the string attached to the seat, so that when the king sat on it the arrow was released and entered his fundament."

 # Wrap it up!

27,000 trees are felled daily to supply the world with toilet paper.

Records show toilet paper being used by the Chinese Emperor way back in 1391. It was a luxury item **for royal asses only**. The paper was made in 2 ft x 3 ft (60 cm x 90 cm) sheets. Such was the demand that The Bureau of Imperial Supplies began producing 720,000 sheets of toilet tissue per year.

Ancient Romans used a **sponge on a stick** kept in a bucket of saltwater. The ancient Jewish practice was to use pebbles or the smooth edges of broken pottery jugs, often carried in a special bag.

In the rest of the world, wealthy people wiped their bums with pieces of wool or lace (imagine!), while **the less fortunate used their hands** and some available water or snow, or they grabbed a handful of leaves and grass, maybe moss, fruit peelings, or corncobs, depending on what the nearby countryside threw up.

Joseph Gayetty introduced packaged toilet tissue to the US in 1857: a 500-sheet pack of **"Therapeutic Paper"** sold for 50¢. It contained aloe to help cure sores and Joe's name was printed on each sheet.

"You got to have smelt a lot of mule manure before you can sing like a hillbilly."

Hank Williams

"The stench of the manure that Jean was turning had cheered him up a little. He adored its promise of fertility and was sniffing it with the relish of a man smelling a randy woman."

Émile Zola, *La Terre*

"WHEN ALL IS SHIT, BECOME A FLY."

Josh Holman

Chapter Three

When Nature Calls

Animal crap facts

Here's a collection of facts from some of the animal kingdom's most successful shitters...

Ever fancied lying on the pristine white sands of a Caribbean beach? Well, a large portion of those shimmering sands are made up of the poo of the **parrot fish**. Each year just one fish can produce up to 200 lbs (90 kg) of sand—more than the weight of your average adult human male.

The **penguin** is a fastidious bird. It backs up to the rim of the family nest, leans forward, and then lets rip, squirting poo at least 24 inches (60 cm) away from the wall of the family nest, thanks to an amazing build-up of rectal pressure. That's up to four times more than any mere human could manage.

Cow dung is pretty powerful stuff. It is known to contain anti-radioactive properties. In the former Soviet Union, people used cow dung to seal their huts from the threat of nuclear fallout.

It's probably no surprise that the **elephant** is one of nature's biggest depositors. Your average elephant can consume between 450–550 lbs (200–250 kg) of food a day. This means when an elephant has to go, it really has to go, and the majestic beast will produce around 110 lbs (50 kg) of crap every single day.

One of the most expensive items on the planet is actually poo. Ambergris, an incredibly pungent material that is valued at tens of thousands of dollars per pound, is in fact poo from the digestive tract of a **sperm whale**. It is highly prized by perfumers because it produces a sweet earthy scent as it ages and also helps the scent of other perfumes to last much longer.

The Nobel Prize for the biggest turd goes to the blue whale at a massive 10 inches (25 cm) wide and several yards long. The bumblebee bat gets the smallest droppings Consolation Cup for its paltry efforts, which measure the size of a pinhead. The Oscar for the smelliest crap goes to… orangutans—but only after eating Durian fruit.

The winner of any projectile-pooping competition has to be the skipper caterpillar, which can launch its poo over 5 ft (1.5 m) in the air—equivalent to around 200 ft (61 m) in human terms. It does this in an effort to fool excrement-guided predators into thinking it is somewhere else.

Captive snakes don't like to mess their living space. Loving owners claim to be able to toilet train their snakes, taking them out in the garden for a crap and then carting them back into captivity. A bright snake could see the makings of an escape plan here.

Sloths, the epitome of laziness, spend all their time hanging out in trees, so you'd imagine that when they need to crap, they'd just let it go. But no! Every week, the sloth creeps very slowly down from its tree and craps on the forest floor. How considerate is that?

Herrings fart as a way of communicating. The bubbles produced by fish farts make a high-frequency sound only audible to other herrings—or so they thought, until the Swedish navy's extra-smart radar mistook a herring chat room session for a Russian submarine.

The intestines of a **horse**, coiled-up obviously, are 89 ft (27 m) long. Horses crap about eight times a day, creating a total of about 35–50 lbs (16–23 kilos) of manure per day. Properly composted, horse manure is a brilliant fertilizer. Also, once you've come in from the garden, why not slip a couple of dried and compressed bricks of horse shit into your wood-burning stove? They burn better and brighter than cured hardwood, or so they say. And don't stop there! Go green and build your house with super-insulating horse manure bricks, or pile fresh manure against the north wall of your house in winter and enjoy the warmth seeping though as the manure decomposes.

One could go on about horse manure, but when you think how much was around before the internal combustion engine, it shouldn't come as much of a surprise. Horse manure changes color and consistency depending on diet. Feasting on grass or bright green hay, the horse will produce a steaming mound of bright green manure that could easily be mistaken for Martian poo. If the horse eats paler green hay, the manure will be paler, and if the poor horse is forced to eat brown hay, the manure will be a similar color. The weather bleaches it all brown in the end, though.

The 2004 Athens Olympic champion horse Shear L'Eau had his manure sold on eBay for a staggering $1500 (over £900).

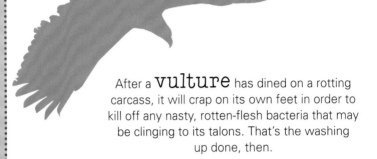

After a **vulture** has dined on a rotting carcass, it will crap on its own feet in order to kill off any nasty, rotten-flesh bacteria that may be clinging to its talons. That's the washing up done, then.

Bat crap is the fertilizer of choice for the home-grown marijuana market, as it contains a high concentration of nitrogen. The droppings have also been processed to produce gunpowder and to make an additive used in laundry detergent. Makes life in the bat cave a bit more interesting, doesn't it, what with all the spliffs, fireworks, and clean underpants.

A prolific pooper, a **rabbit** can produce more than 500 pellets a day. And they don't mind eating them—in fact, they quite like it.

Do not invite a $goose$ into your home.
It will crap, messily, about once every
10 minutes.

Another $elephant$ crap fact:
they do eat shit. In fact, they stick
their trunks right up each other's
asses so as not to waste time.
Animals who eat their own poo do
so because they have less-than-efficient digestive
systems and what comes out still has nutrients in it
worthy of another go-round. But I'm sure Dumbo
didn't do that kind of thing.

You could invite a $bear$ to come and
hibernate in your spare room, however, and
you wouldn't even have to change the
sheets. An internal plug of poo and hair
bungs up the bear for the duration.

Male **hippos** have a charming way of making their presence felt and smelt. Their tail acts as a whirling rotor blade, so when they back out of the water ready to get all seductive, they crap and whirr, spraying sloppy hippo shit as far and wide as possible. Less a case of the shit hitting the fan, more like the fan hitting the shit—but with the same distressing result.

A **palm civet** is a species of wild cat that hangs out in the jungles of Southeast Asia and has exclusive enzymes in its stomach that can turn a coffee berry into a bean that, once excreted, washed, and roasted, tastes of caramel. The resulting coffee is called kopi luwak and can cost up to $240 (£145) per pound. It's not a nice trade, though—at that price, civets are often battery farmed for their crap. Wrong.

Wombat shit is interesting. Well, quite interesting in a fit-for-purpose sort of way. They crap square pellets so they can use them to mark out territory and advertise their presence—for them, crap is rather like a primitive sat-nav. And, as their territory is basically rock- and log-strewn bush country, the crap cubes stay just where they pooped them. If wombat crap pellets were rounded, like those of koalas, they would probably roll off the intended GPS point and confuse friends and family no end.

An exhaustive study of more than 70 **dogs** from 37 breeds showed that they prefer to crap with their bodies aligned on a north-south axis, in line with the Earth's magnetic field, and they actively avoid crapping in an east-west direction. Handy to know if you've forgotten your compass.

"Dogs are animals that poo in public and you're supposed to pick it up. After a week of doing this, you've got to ask yourself, 'Who's the real master in this relationship?'"

Anthony Griffin

Animal crap anecdotes

Animals use their crap to leave messages: I'm here, be afraid; I'm here, come and get me baby!; or I've crapped, so pick it up!

Every crap tells a story

Want to be an ace animal crap detective? Take notes. Hunters and wildlife experts can look at a mound of dung, analyze how fresh it is and what's in it, and then identify the animal and the direction in which it went.

First off, you'll want to know if the mess at your feet comes from a carnivore or herbivore.

Vegetarian shit is generally compact and geometric, like the rounded pellets made by deer and rabbits. The size is proportional to that of the animal that produced it, so deer pellets will be smaller than those produced by a massive moose.

Carnivores' crap is, on the whole, messier and smellier, and can contain bits of fur, bone, and feathers.

A tip:

If you come across a massive pile of fresh, steaming dung containing a pair of half-digested binoculars and the remains of a safari jacket, you'll probably be okay because the beast will be away somewhere sleeping off its lunch.

The dog ate my tax money!

Apparently, a certain Wayne Klinkel from Montana left his one-eyed golden retriever Sundance in the car while he went off for lunch. Also in the car was a wad of five $100 notes in the glove box (let's not speculate about why Wayne stashes cash in his glove box). He came back from lunch to find Sundance licking his lips, a shred of chewed up $100 bill stuck to his lips. Every day for the next couple of weeks Wayne tracked the one-eyed hound, collecting his crap in a plastic bag. Wayne kept his collection of dog mess frozen in the cold outside his house, until the day came to thaw the poo in a bucket of soapy water. Using an old metal mining screen and a hose, he separated out the $100 bill fragments, washed and assembled them like so many jigsaw puzzles, and sent them off to the U.S. Treasury. Six months later, the Mutilated Currency Division sent him a cheque for $500. Luckily Sundance did not get to the mailbox before his owner. All of which proves that persistence pays off and that U.S. Treasury bank notes contain a lot of indigestible fiber.

Horse manure in history

In the first Defenestration of Prague in 1419, an angry mob stormed into Prague Castle, made their way up to the third floor where the Council were in session, and threw the lot of them to their deaths from the (conveniently large) window. The Second Defenestration of Prague occurred in 1618. This time the ruling Protestants threw four Catholic Lords out of the window, only to find that they survived because they landed in a nice, warm heap of horse manure. As a result, the argument never really got resolved and basically resulted in the Thirty Years' War. Only don't quote me on this, especially not in an exam paper.

✒

Forget the gold rush...

Seabird crap, known as guano, with its high phosphate and nitrogen levels, is the ultimate miracle fertilizer and worth a fortune. It's been fertilizing South American crops since Inca times. The prize producer is the Guanay Cormorant, or Shag, a resident of Peru and Chile. Some outlying uninhabited islands in the Pacific are practically made of guano, and in the 18th and 19th centuries land-grab treaties, legal challenges, undignified skirmishes, and wars were fought over the rights to mine the shit. In fact, the USA still owns about a dozen Guano Islands in the North Pacific.

"Never kick a fresh turd on a hot day."

Anthony Griffin

A fanciful tale

In the 16th and 17th centuries, everything had to be transported by ship, and large shipments of the miracle fertilizer manure were common. It was shipped dry, because in this form it weighed a lot less than when it was wet, but, once water seeped into a ship's hold, it became heavier and the process of fermentation began again, of which methane gas, as every schoolkid knows, is a by-product.

As the stuff was stored below decks in bundles you can guess what could (and did) happen. Methane began to build up, and the first time someone came below at night with a lantern…
BOOOOM!

Several ships were destroyed in this manner before the penny dropped. After that, bundles of manure were stamped with the term "Ship High In Transit," instructing the sailors to stow manure bricks on upper decks so that water seeping into the hold would not touch the volatile cargo.

Thus evolved the term **S.H.I.T.** Or not, as actually the word shit derives from the Old Norse word *skita*, which is used to describe cows with diarrhea. Nice story, though.

"Spontaneously, without any theological training, I, a child, grasped the incompatibility of God and shit and thus came to question the basic thesis of Christian anthropology, namely that man was created in God's image. Either/or: either man was created in God's image—and has intestines!—or God lacks intestines and man is not like him.

The ancient Gnostics felt as I did at the age of five. In the second century, the Great Gnostic master Valentinus resolved the damnable dilemma by claiming that Jesus 'ate and drank, but did not defecate."

Milan Kundera, *The Unbearable Lightness of Being*

"Who his foul tail with paper wipes, shall at his ballocks leave some chips."

François Rabelais, *Gargantua and Pantagruel*

Chapter Four

Cultural Crap

Crap films

We've all sat through a film and said: "This is shit." The following crap-based movie scenes genuinely live up to that statement.

TOP CRAP-COATED MOVIE MOMENTS

Check out the highest-grossing Norwegian film of all time, **Headhunters**, based on Jo Nesbø's book of the same name—specifically the scene in the outhouse, when protagonist Roger hides from his nemesis, the crazy psychopath Clas, by immersing himself completely in the dung pit and using the cardboard center of a loo roll as a breathing tube. Would death at the hands of a madman be preferable?

Jamal, the young hero of **Slumdog Millionaire**, is trapped in a latrine by his controlling elder brother. Desperate to get the autograph of a visiting film star, Jamal takes a dive into the cesspit, ultimately emerging covered in shit but still clutching the crumpled picture of his hero, who then gives him his hard-won signature. A clue to the tenacity of our Slumdog.

MEANINGFUL MOVIE MOMENTS

There are plenty of reasons why tense and nasty moments in movies are staged in lavatories: they are supposed to be private places so people are off their guard, there are places to hide, there's a nice echo to the gunshots, and blood looks very dramatic splashed about on the tiles. Directors like to send us meaningful messages from the toilet block. Here are a few:

In **Jurassic Park**, a rampaging T-Rex smashes down a toilet block before plucking lawyer Donald Gennaro off the loo and devouring him in one bite. Must have some message for the legal profession.

A scene in **Trainspotting** sees Renton diving into a shitty toilet bowl in an effort to retrieve his opium suppositories, only to emerge into a beautiful sunlit underwater world... before ultimately returning to the shit. Pretty much sums up the life of an addict.

Quentin Tarantino's **Pulp Fiction** is a wonderfully dense film of intersecting storylines about LA mobsters, where scenes set in toilets signal something bad is about to happen. Mobster Vincent Vega, on a mission to murder a character called Butch, waits for his victim to return to his apartment. He carelessly puts down his machine pistol in the kitchen and goes for a crap. Butch returns home and, thinking he's got time for a snack, puts a couple of pop tarts in the toaster. Vincent flushes and emerges, only to find that Butch now has the gun. The pop tarts pop up as Butch lets Vincent have it. This is how it goes for the average mobster—life's not worth a shit.

A quick canter through crap literature

If anyone tries to tell you that crap, poo, and fart jokes are the stuff of uneducated minds, time to wheel out the literary heavyweights.

The first recorded fart joke was scrawled on a Sumerian tablet about 2,000 years B.C. about the way young women always deny that they fart. It's the way they tell them.

In **Aristophanes' *The Clouds*** (423 B.C.), one character gives another a bit too much information about his bowel movements: "I get colic, then the stew sets to rumbling like thunder and finally bursts forth with a terrific noise."

In **Dante Alighieri's *Inferno***, a journey through hell written in 1300, a demon mobilizes his troops by using "his ass as a trumpet."

In **Rabelais' *Pantagruel*** (1532) the giant, Pantagruel, releases a fart that "made the earth shake for twenty-nine miles around, and the foul air he blew out created more than fifty-three thousand tiny men, dwarves, and creatures of weird shapes, and then he emitted a fat wet fart that turned into just as many tiny stooping women."

Chaucer's *The Miller's Tale* was written in the 1380s. It's about two young men, Nicholas and Absolon, both vying for the favors of fair Alisoun who is married to John, an older man. Nicholas has tricked John into spending the night in a tub halfway up a tree (don't ask), leaving the way clear for him to make his move. Nicholas is in bed with Alisoun and jealous Absolon is hanging about outside the bedroom window. Nicholas decides it's time to teach the stalker a lesson:

"And so he opened window hastily,
And put his arse out thereat, quietly,
Over the buttocks, showing the whole bum;
And thereto said this clerk, this Absolon,
'O speak, sweet bird, I know not where thou art.'
This Nicholas just then let fly a fart
As loud as it had been a thunder-clap,
And well-nigh blinded Absolon, poor chap."

Lots of fart jokes in Shakespeare. Here's a line from
A Comedy of Errors (1594):

A man may break a word with you, sir; and words are but wind; Ay, and break it in your face, so he break it not behind.

From **John Aubrey's *Brief Lives*** (1680): "The Earl of Oxford, making of his low obeisance to Queen Elizabeth, happened to let a fart, at which he was so abashed and ashamed that he went to travel seven years. On his return the Queen said: 'My lord. We have forgot the fart.'"

❧

Benjamin Franklin, in response to a call from The Royal Academy of Science for serious scientific papers, jokingly suggested that scientists should use their skills to develop a way to make farts into perfumed air.

❧

Jonathan Swift, best known as the author of *Gulliver's Travels*, published ***The Benefit of Farting*** in 1722. "I take it there are five or six different species of fart." These are "the sonorous and full-toned or rousing fart," "the double fart," "the soft fizzing fart," "the wet fart," and "the sullen wind-bound fart."

❧

In chapter four of **James Joyce's *Ulysses*** (1922), Leopold Bloom has a crap that lasts for four pages. "He felt full, heavy: then a gentle loosening of his bowels. He stood up undoing the waistband of his trousers … A paper. He liked to read at stool … In the drawer he found an old number of Titbits." And on and on it goes, via "asquat the cuckstool … seated calm above his own rising smell," until the climax we've all been waiting for: "He tore away half the prize story sharply and wiped himself with it, then he girded up his trousers, braced and buttoned himself. He pulled back the jerky shaky door of the jakes and came forth from the gloom into the air."

❧

South Park (1997 onward). Pick just about any episode, and if there is no mention of farts or toilets complain to your TV station.

❦ Poetry corner ❧

Forget hosts of golden daffodils, waving and
drowning, corners of foreign fields, and all
that romantic and meaningful versifying.
Farting is a splendid topic for the poet, as is
evidenced here.

The Farter from Sparta

There was a young fellow from Sparta,
A really magnificent farter.
On the strength of one bean
He'd fart 'God Save the Queen,'
And Beethoven's Moonlight Sonata.
He could vary, with proper persuasion,
His fart to suit any occasion.
He could fart like a flute,
Like a lark, like a lute,
This highly fartistic Caucasian.
This sparkling young farter from Sparta,
His fart for no money would barter.
He could roar from his rear
Any scene from Shakespeare,
Or Gilbert and Sullivan's Mikado.
Nobody could play the classics finer,
As he showed me one day in the diner.
I had a bagel with lox
While he played from his buttocks:
Chopin's Etude #12 in C-minor.

He'd fart a gavotte for a starter,
And fizzle a fine serenata.
He could play on his anus
The Coriolanus;
Oof, boom,er-tum,tootle, yum tah-dah!
He was great in the Christmas Cantata,
He could double-stop fart the Toccata,
He'd boom from his ass
Bach's B-Minor Mass,
And in counterpoint, La Traviata.
Spurred on by a very high wager
With an envious German named Bager,
He'd proceeded to fart
The complete oboe part
Of a Haydn Octet in B-major.
His repertoire ranged from classics to jazz,
He achieved new effects with bubbles of gas.
With a good dose of salts
He could whistle a waltz
Or swing it in razzamatazz.
His basso profundo with timbre so rare
He rendered quite often, with power to spare.
But his great work of art,
His fortissimo fart,
He saved for the Marche Militaire.
One day he was dared to perform
The William Tell Overture Storm,
But naught could dishearten
Our spirited Spartan,
For his fart was in wonderful form.
It went off in capital style,

And he farted it through with a smile,
Then, feeling quite jolly,
He tried the finale,
Blowing double-stopped farts all the while.
The selection was tough, I admit,
But it did not dismay him one bit,
Then, with his ass thrown aloft
He suddenly coughed...
And collapsed in a shower of shit.
His bunghole was blown back to Sparta,
Where they buried the rest of our farter,
With a gravestone of turds
Inscribed with the words:
"To the Fine Art of Farting, A Martyr."

THE YOUNG GIRL OF LA PLATA

There was a young girl of La Plata
Who was widely renowned as a farter.
Her deafening reports
At the Argentine sports
Made her much in demand as a starter.

A FART CAN BE USEFUL

A fart can be useful;
It gives the body ease,
It warms the bed in winter
And suffocates the fleas.

Crap art

Who paints shit? Or more specifically: why?
Here's a probable answer:

"In the Renaissance the artist was thought to be
a kind of god, and art was thought to spring from
his reflective brow… suggesting that art was
imbued with 'ancient wisdom' and a 'sacred
trust,' but [and here he names a couple of 'new
shit artists,' one of them being Paul McCarthy]
show that the artist has become an unreflective
asshole, and art has been dumbed down…
to mindless shit, that most leveling
and un-ideal of all substances."

Donald Kuspit,
Professor of Art History and Philosophy

The Father of Pop Art, **Richard Hamilton**, took a trip down this
path. He found a cache of old postcards from the French village
of Miers, which showed a group of people, skirts up and
trousers down, crapping together in a country lane in celebration
of the beneficial laxative effects of the local water. He turned the
images into a series of paintings, culminating in a small etching
and aquatint (edition of 100) of a touchingly neat little turd,
entitled *Un des effets des eaux de Miers*. One was auctioned
recently for around $1250 (£750).

Now we come to the most monstrous shit of all: **Complex Shit**—a giant inflatable 51-ft (15-m) high massive turd created by American contemporary artist **Paul McCarthy** (see opinion on page 61). In 2008 it was installed in a park in Bern, Switzerland, but unfortunately it came loose from its moorings during strong winds and subsequently bought down a power line before eventually crashing through the windows of several nearby buildings. In 2013 it was on display in Hong Kong and was totally destroyed by torrential rain. That's muscular art criticism for you.

In further shit-fueled japes, McCarthy collaborated with fellow artist **Jason Rhoades** on a installation entitled Propposition. While displaying the installation in Hamburg, two fellow artists Benne Ender and Jan Northoff decided to present Rhoades with a thoughtful gift: a pile of crap gathered together from the toilets of the *documenta* contemporary art exhibition. Touched by such a kind gesture, McCarthy and Rhoades decided to encase the crap in giant butt plugs to display at their 2002 exhibition **Shit Plug**.

Piero Manzoni had a big idea way back in 1961. He produced 90 small tin cans, each of which was filled with his own shit and labeled helpfully in several languages:

> **Artist's Shit**
> **Contents 30 gr net**
> **Freshly preserved**
> **Produced and tinned**
> **in May 1961**

The idea was to sell them at the current rate per gram of gold. One can sold for $124,000 (almost £75,000) in 2008. Some say they are filled with plaster, but at that price, who's going to open one to find out? In the mid-1990s an art collector called John Hunov sued a museum in Denmark for causing leakage to a can he'd loaned for display by storing it at "irresponsibly warm temperatures." And he won, ultimately being awarded a payout of 250,000 Danish Krone (over $45,000/£27,000).

Mary Kelly, a feminist artist whose work consists mainly of "narrative installations," caused a bit of a stir with an exhibition at the ICA in London in 1976. It consisted, in part, of a collection of her baby son's stained nappy liners, carefully framed in Perspex boxes. How the mother/son relationship progressed from there is a matter of conjecture.

Acknowledgments

I would like to dedicate this book to the person who said: "Whatever you do, don't dedicate your crap book to me."

A Friendly Piece of Advice:
Diagnosed early, diseases of the bowel can be treated and the outcome is good. Get to know your body and its regular habits. If you find blood in your poo, suffer unexplained weight loss, constant constipation, or diarrhea, then consult your doctor immediately.